THE WONDER AND BEAUTY OF WESTONBIRT

Graham Light

Foreword by
HRH The Duchess of Cornwall

ACER PRESS LIMITED

First published 2010 by Acer Press Ltd.,
17c/d Village Farm, Preston, Cirencester,
Gloucestershire, GL7 5PR.

A catalogue record for this book is
available from the British Library.

ISBN 978-0-9566631-0-8

Printed in the UK by

Butler Tanner & Dennis

ACER PRESS LIMITED

Contents

Foreword   4

Introduction   5

Spring   7

Summer   46

Autumn   86

Winter   127

Map   151

Foreword by Her Royal Highness The Duchess of Cornwall

'Getty Images©'

Westonbirt the National Arboretum is an extraordinary collection of trees, set in a landscape of woodland vistas. Under the canopy of mature trees, skilful groupings of smaller trees and shrubs form a backdrop to swathes of woodland flowers.

As Westonbirt's next-door neighbour, I have always admired its roadside view, which intrigues as it offers glimpses of fiery foliage in autumn or peaceful green glades in summer. I was therefore delighted to be asked to be Patron to the Friends of Westonbirt Arboretum and discover more intimately the popular highlights, as well as the secret corners of the Arboretum. The Friends of Westonbirt Arboretum provide considerable and wide-ranging support to the Forestry Commission, and I am therefore enormously encouraged that the Friends will benefit from the sale of this book.

I am delighted that this book encourages a wider appreciation of the Arboretum by focusing on the different seasons. Whether you prefer a gentle stroll, a guided walk, or just the chance to sit and ponder, the photographs of Graham Light will draw your eye to new wonders.

INTRODUCTION

For me, the National Arboretum at Westonbirt is a wonderful place to visit all year round. It is perhaps most famous for its display of autumnal colour reflecting the vibrancy and deepening reds of the maples. However, after spending more than three years visiting the arboretum to record its ever changing hues, I have become even more convinced of its beauty at any time of the year.

No matter when you come and no matter the weather there is always something worth exploring and to photograph.

This is a book of how I, as a professional photographer, view Westonbirt. I spend my time looking for shapes, tones, colours, silhouettes, interesting and unusual angles as well as the more familiar viewpoints. For me, it is recording it as I see it and as I want to show you. It is also about encouraging you to come at other times of the year and for you to see for yourself the many changes I have captured here. Even now, though I have completed my photography for the purposes of this book, I return on a regular basis to enjoy what Westonbirt offers.

I suppose we all have our favourite places or favourite tree. I just love the all encompassing nature of the champion tree *Betula ermanii* (Erman's birch), found along Mitchell Drive a short distance from Mitchell Gate, as it displays different aspects and characteristics throughout the year.

We begin in the spring when the arboretum comes alive with a carpet of wild flowers especially in Silk Wood. In the Old Arboretum we have the rhododendrons, azaleas and camellias along with cherries, magnolias and a variety of other species coming into full bloom. This great show of colour brings a feeling of well-being as we see spring coming into its own. This book then takes you through the seasons, sometimes on dull overcast days, and sometimes on bright and vibrant days, to expose you to the many treasures and magical moments we can all enjoy throughout the year here at Westonbirt.

Whether you decide to take a casual stroll through the Old Arboretum or a prolonged walk into Silk Wood you will find that Westonbirt has much to offer individuals and families and those who want to exercise their dog (restricted to Silk Wood and The Downs).

The Old Arboretum provides the photographer in me with plenty of opportunities to be imaginative and creative in my approach. I just love the shapes often provided by the various maple trees and rhododendrons, the emerging buds and new leaves with their bright fresh green colours and from time to time the opportunity to shoot into the light with the resultant images capturing the beautiful silhouettes and shapes produced by the various trees. With every turn along the way there is something new to attract the photographer and visitor alike. For a wonderful show of bluebells you need only to walk through Silk Wood to come across groups of these native flowers. Often large displays that carpet the woodland create a mist of blue as far as the eye can see.

As we move into summer we see trees in full leaf and many parts of the arboretum sheltering under the canopy these leaves provide. A number of the specimen trees really come into their own at this time of year, showing off their vast displays of leaves and flowers. Children are able to enjoy both the fun and games of following various trails set out for them or by visiting the play area for the younger children adjacent to the visitors services and the outdoor cafe.

Autumn is ablaze with a riot of colour from the maples as well as many of our native trees and it is at this time of year that Westonbirt attracts the majority of its visitors. However, if that is the only time of the year you visit you are missing out on a wonderful spectacle that can be enjoyed throughout the year. It is my hope that this book will inspire you to visit the arboretum throughout the year and at the same time bring inspiration to your photography as you capture the scenes that unfold before you.

Winter brings its own challenges to the visitor and photographer at Westonbirt. You may have to overcome the cold, contend with limited daylight hours and often work and visit under dull, overcast conditions. But do not let that deter you from visiting as there is so much to see and appreciate in the winter months. Sometimes we are surprised at the emergence of bright bold flowers that suddenly appear, there are quite a few varieties that will be in full bloom in January. We may have the benefit of a hoar frost that leaves its mark across the arboretum creating a magical feel or a blanket of snow will cover the landscape transforming the arboretum into a winter wonderland. Often the weather will be kind and many a day can be spent enjoying beautiful blue skies and bright sunshine on a crisp and fresh day and it is a joy to explore, breaking the walk for a warm coffee in Maples Restaurant.

I have endeavoured to be as accurate as possible in identifying both the species and the locations, but it is possible that you may find one or two that are incorrect and if that is the case please do accept my apologies.

For those of you interested in the technical side of my photography I provide the following information on shutter speeds, apertures and ISO setting used on a few of the images:
Front cover: ISO 400, focal length 24 mm, f4.8, 1/90 second.
Back cover: ISO 200, focal length 24 mm, f11, 1/80 second.
Front end papers: ISO 100, focal length 28 mm, f5.6, 1/80 second.
Back end papers: ISO 100, focal length 19 mm, f13, 1/10 second.
Contents page: ISO 400, focal length 24 mm, f4.5, 1/80 second.
Title page: ISO 200, focal length 24 mm, f4.8, 1/90 second.
All the photographs in this book were taken on Nikon Digital SLR cameras using either a Nikon D200, Nikon D2X or Nikon D3 and the lenses employed were a combination of Nikon 24 -120 mm, Nikon 12 - 24 mm, Nikon 16 - 35 mm and Nikon 28 - 105 mm macro. All images were recorded as RAW files and post capture processing was carried out in Adobe Photoshop.

Images from the book are available to order as framed prints, on canvas or other media as required. To order or commission other work contact Graham by e-mail on consult@abbey-studios.co.uk or telephone the studio on 01285 653069. www.abbey-studios.co.uk and www.abbeyphotoschool.co.uk

I would like to express my appreciation to Her Royal Highness The Duchess of Cornwall for consenting to write the Foreword for this book as a Patron of The Friends of Westonbirt Arboretum.

I am deeply grateful to the support, help, advice and encouragement I have received from many of the staff and volunteers at Westonbirt including Simon Toomer, Hugh Angus, Ben Jones, Louisa Lockwood, Mike & Rosemary Westgate, Diana East and others who are too numerous to mention. I am also grateful for the encouragement and support I have had from my wife Gloria, without her encouragement this book may never have come to fruition.

The Friends of Westonbirt Arboretum provide a much needed and valued support for the arboretum, for full details of membership, its benefits and how you can get involved go to their website at www.fowa.org.uk or talk to a volunteer when visiting, you will find some on duty in the Great Oak Hall.

Some of the proceeds from the sale of each book will be donated to the Friends of Westonbirt Arboretum.

For information on Westonbirt, The National Arboretum, see www.forestry.gov.uk/westonbirt or www.westonbirtarboretum.com

Graham Light, LBIPP.

Above: Forsythia

Above: Erman's birch

Above: Cherry

Champion tree, Erman's birch, spreads out its branches to welcome in spring and all around we begin to see signs of new life appearing. Much that has been dormant through the winter period is now beginning to emerge.

Left: Magnolia

Above: Maple

Left: Winter's bark

Right: Magnolia stellata

The undergrowth of the arboretum begins to unveil the variety of wild flowers and blossom, each of which encourages us to see even better days ahead as winter passes and spring emerges.

Left: Wood anemone

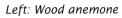

Above: Wild cherry

Above: Lesser celandine

Left: Blue anemone

Above: Primrose

Above: Indian plum

Above: Sargent's cherry

Above: A woodland walk in Silk Wood

Above: Cherry blossom
Left: Magnolia

Above: Magnolia

Right: Berberis
Far right: Broad Drive, Silk Wood

9

Above: The Downs from Downs track
Left: Stachyurus praecox

Volunteering at Westonbirt enables you to engage in numerous activities which in the past has included the restoration of this ha ha wall on the Downs Link near the Great Oak Hall.

Above: Restored ha ha wall, Downs Link near Main Drive

Below: Waste Drive, Silk Wood

Above: Sargent's cherry, Broad Drive, Silk Wood

Above: Camellia

Main Drive and Savill Glade offer up a wonderful display of colour as camellia and magnolia open up their spectacular blooms.

Above: Camellia

Above left and centre: Main Drive and Savill Glade, Old Arboretum

Left and above: Camellia

Right: Magnolia campbellii

11

Magnolia sprengeri *'diva'* in all her glory,
Circular Drive, Old Arboretum.

Above: Entrance to the Old Arboretum, Downs Link near the Great Oak Hall

Below and right:The Downs Link close to the Old Arboretum entrance adjoining the Great Oak Hall

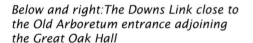

Below: Birches on the Downs Link

Many of our native trees are to be enjoyed on the Downs Link. The glass sculptures have now gone to the Forest of Dean but were quite a feature in the landscape of the Downs Link for the time they were here.

Above: Magnolia

Above and below: The Downs

Above: White barked Himalayan birch, Pool Gate, The Downs

Above: Dew pond near Pool Gate, Old Arboretum

The restored dew pond can be located near to Pool Gate. Nearby the white barked Himalayan birch stands out in contrast to the darker backdrop of the Old Arboretum.

Sunlight highlights this maple, *Acer palmatum*, along Main Drive. The landscape as viewed from Main Drive through Pool Gate creates the opportunity for some creative photography as it brings together a number of elements in the image for the good of the whole.

Above: Acer palmatum, Main Drive, Old Arboretum

Left: Specimen and Main Drive, close to the dew pond Old Arboretum

Inset left to right: Magnolia, holly and cherry

Left: Pool Gate, Old Arboretum

Below: Magnolia

15

Above: Wellingtonia, Main Drive
Old Arboretum

Left and above: Western red cedar, Main Drive,
Old Arboretum

The curves of the western red cedars are emphasised by the low angle of the sunlight. The gate featured in this shot of Dukes Cut Gate adds scale and interest to the photograph.

Right: Dukes Cut Gate,
Old Arboretum

Left: Hornbeam maple

Above : Rhododendron

Above: Rhododendron

Above and below right: Prunus shogetsu, Japanese flowering cherry

When the light is played on the seed heads and flowers we are able to create some interesting views of these subjects.Being observant brings many benefits as it is all too easy to pass by some of these interesting plants and viewpoints.

Below :Great white cherry

Below: Magnolia

Above: Oak, The Downs

Above: Restored ha ha wall Dukes Cut Gate, Old Arboretum

Above: Dukes Cut Gate

Round every corner there is something new to observe and enjoy, be it the wide open spaces of The Downs, the long straight view as we glance along Savill Glade or the carpet of colour formed by falling petals from many of the flowering trees and shrubs. Take time to sit, relax and enjoy them on one of the many benches provided.

Left and right: The Old Arboretum

Above: View from Main Drive to the Downs behind you

Left: Savill Glade

Above: Blue anemone

Above: Japanese maple

Above: Downs Link near the Great Oak Hall

Right: Horse and sweet chestnuts, Downs Link

Above: Magnolia

A keen eye and observant nature will enable you to see and enjoy many of these spectacles as the light plays on them at different times of the day.

Right: Magnolia 'Alba superba'

The strong blue of this sky is just as it was with no enhancement or use of filters. Sometimes nature has a wonderful way of bringing all the elements together and all we have to do is interpret them, select the correct viewpoint and capture the image. Here, in addition to the blue sky, the horizon has a line of white cloud behind the fencing, creating a separation between the green of The Downs and the blue of the sky.

Above: Beech on The Downs
Left: Birch in the Valley, Silk Wood

Above: Woodland walk in Silk Wood

Left: Timber management in Silk Wood

Below: Bluebells

Above: Wood anemone

Silk Wood provides opportunities to be away from the hustle and bustle of life and to enjoy nature at its very best. Follow the native tree trail from Skilling Gate and you will come across this fun feature about our native oaks.

Right: Native tree trail in Silk Wood near Skilling Gate

Spring in Silk Wood is welcomed by a carpet of wild flowers especially along Palmer Ride.

All: Various views around Palmer Ride carpeted with wild flowers in spring. Many of our native trees can found in this area.

As you travel along Palmer Ride you are able to enjoy the new fresh green shoots emerging on many of the trees. These greens are often highlighted as you view them with the benefit of back lighting from the sun. Sometimes it pays to change our viewpoint for a different perspective and look heavenward into the canopy that is gradually unfolding.

All: Palmer Ride in Silk Wood contains a wonderful collection of our native trees which on a bright spring day catch the sunlight and highlight the foliage.

Above: Dwarf buckeye found in Silk Wood

Left: Native Oak, Palmer Ride, Silk Wood

The Dwarf buckeye reawakens earlier than many other species and here at Westonbirt we quickly observe the bright red nature of those emerging shoots especially as they contrast with the yellow of the celandines breaking into flower around them.

Above: Dwarf buckeye and celandines

Right: Palmer Ride, Silk Wood

Right: Palmer Ride/ Waste Drive with the craft shelter

Below: Many of the trees display an attractive bark

Above and below: Beech trees near Skilling Gate

I love the variety and textures of the bark on many of the trees to be found around Westonbirt as they provide an interesting study in themselves. The beech trees near Skilling Gate offer shade, shelter and colour throughout the year.

Above: Native trees in Silk Wood

I found this full moon maple in Silk Wood and it provided me with many opportunities to use the light to capture its beauty in a variety of ways. Not only are the flowers attractive but so are the leaves especially with the benefit of back lighting provided by the sun.

All: Full moon maple (Acer japonicum) looking spectacular with the sunlight emphasing its beauty and delicate nature of the flowers.

Above: Native bluebells

At this time of year the rhododendrons and magnolias put on a display of their own and can be seen at various locations around the arboretum.

Above, left and bottom right: A carpet of rhododendron petals, Main Drive, Old Arboretum

Above: Magnolia

Above: Cowslips on The Downs near Waste Gate

Above: The Downs along Downs track

Above: The Downs from Downs track

The Downs themselves play host to many cowslips and other wild flowers which contrast greatly against the fresh green grass of spring. The hawthorns also begin to flourish and have a wonderful display of delicate white flowers tinged with pink as they emerge.

Above: On The Downs a hawthorn in full bloom

Above - Flowering Cherry along Downs track

Right: From Waste Gate looking along the valley to The Downs

Above and below centre: Cowslips, bluebells and a variety of wild flowers are in abundance

Above: Downs track towards Waste Gate

Below: Native bluebells border a woodland walk in Silk Wood

Below: Native bluebells in Silk Wood

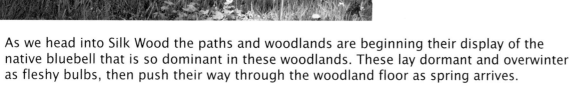

As we head into Silk Wood the paths and woodlands are beginning their display of the native bluebell that is so dominant in these woodlands. These lay dormant and overwinter as fleshy bulbs, then push their way through the woodland floor as spring arrives.

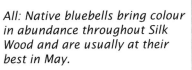

All: Native bluebells bring colour in abundance throughout Silk Wood and are usually at their best in May.

The bluebell emerges with a host of small flowers along each stem. After pollination these flowers quickly die, but in the meantime form a carpet of blue beneath the woodlands and often appear as a mist of blue in the distant view. By actively managing the woodland, West onbirt ensures that these native flowers will continue to be with us for many years to come.

Left: Savill Glade with its display of colour from the numerous rhododendrons and azaleas to be found there

Left and above: Rhododendron luteum also known as the honeysuckle azalea

Above: Fungus, Dryad's Saddle

Amidst the glorious display from the rhododendron, azalea and magnolia we discover one of the many fungi to be found around Westonbirt.

Above: Magnolia

Left: The National Japanese Maple collection can be found around Maple Loop

Above and centre: Some of the many attractive walks to be found off Rotary Glade

As you walk around Rotary Glade, Maple Loop and the National Japanese Maple Collection, you will see bluebells emerging in the woodland and they provide a striking contrast in colour to the vibrant red and golden hues of the young maple leaves.

Left and right: Native bluebells carpet the woodland floor and contrast with the Japanese maples

All: The Japanese Maple Collection is found in Silk Wood around Rotary Glade. The backdrop of the maples emphasise the strong blue from the native bluebells in the foreground

Bluebells dominate the foreground and the sun draws attention to the striking colours of the fresh new leaves of the maples. The theme continues around Rotary Glade where there is so much evidence of spring bordering into what is soon to be summer.

All: Silk Wood where maples and native bluebells are in abundance around Rotary Glade and Maple Loop,

The National Japanese Maple Collection plays host to many varieties and their delicate yet striking leaves are a riot of colour at this time of year.

Above: Close to The Link in Silk Wood where walking the dog is a regular activity

Above: Woodland walks abound in Silk Wood

If you are looking for a combination of broad vistas and quiet woodland walks where you can relax and exercise your dog then Silk Wood is a must to explore. Broad Drive is bordered on both sides with open grassland and a backdrop of trees and shrubs that offer a vast array of colour, form, shape and texture whereas many of the woodland walks offer shade and solitude accompanied by many woodland and wild flowers.

Above: Broad Drive in Silk Wood with its wide and varied collection of trees

All: Close to The Link and Willesley Drive the landscape is once again carpeted with native bluebells which flourish in the dappled sunlight of Silk Wood

Above: Dandelion seed heads backlit by the sun

Above: The Downs

Above: Main Drive, Old Arboretum

Below: Rhododendron

Below: Azaleas

Above: A quiet spot in Silk Wood

Wherever you are in the arboretum there is always plenty to see and enjoy, be it the rolling slopes of The Downs offering up their contribution of wildflowers, the azaleas and rhododendron to be found in the Old Arboretum or a quiet spot in Silk Wood to sit and relax and take in the beauty of nature.

All: Main Drive and Savill Glade in the Old Arboretum where azaleas and rhododendrons flower profusely

All: Savill Glade, Old Arboretum, alive with the colours of rhododendron, azalea and native bluebells

Colours and shapes, shadows and texture, all are to be found as you walk around and explore the Old Arboretum.

39

Above: A quiet resting place on Circular Drive, Old Arboretum

Interest is provided throughout spring by the profuse display of flowers such as rhododendron, azalea and magnolia.

All: Circular Drive, Old Arboretum with its display of magnolia, rhododendron and azaleas

Above and right: Native bluebells nestle under the trees along
Loop Walk, Old Arboretum

Above: Loop Walk

Above: Loop Walk in the Old Arboretum

Right: Azalea

41

Above: Loop Walk, Old Arboretum

Above: Looking down Holford Ride towards Westonbirt School

Below: Holford Ride at its junction with Pool Avenue, Old Arboretum

Above: Pool Avenue as it meets Holford Ride

From Holford Ride we take in the view of the mansion house which now houses Westonbirt School. The ride was one of many that radiated from the house to provide spectacular views of the arboretum. Today we are able to enjoy that view in reverse order and observe how the mansion sits so comfortably in this landscape.

Above: Cedar of Lebanon, Pool Gate, Old Arboretum

Above: The Handkerchief Tree (Davidia involucrata)

Below: Wellingtonia and rhododendron on Main Drive, Old Arboretum

Below: Off Main Drive, Old Arboretum

Not only do we observe the 'expected' displays from rhododendrons and azaleas but the keen observer will also spot the unusual Handkerchief Tree especially around Main Drive and Loop Walk of the Old Arboretum. It is also to be found in parts of Silk Wood.

Above and below: native bluebells adjoining the Cherry Collection in Silk Wood

Above: Bluebells contrast with dandelions along Broad Drive in Silk Wood

A carpet of dandelions along Broad Drive lead us to a thin line on the horizon created by the bluebells that border the woodland. At the same time, a short walk away, the Cherry Collection is also in full bloom with a show of wildflowers underneath.

Right : The Cherry Collection in Silk Wood

Above: Main Drive,
Old Arboretum

Above: Acer palmatum catching the sunlight, Main Drive

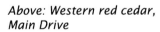

Above: Western red cedar,
Main Drive

The fresh green tones of
the new seasons growth
are highlighted by the
dappled light and occasional
contrast of flowering trees
and shrubs.

Above: Magnolia on Main Drive

Right: Azalea

45

Above: Erman's birch, Mitchell Drive

I am captivated by this champion tree, it was planted in the 1850s by the Holford family as they were setting out their arboretum here at Westonbirt. When last measured in 2002 the height was 22 metres with a girth of 390 cm. and a diameter of 124 cm. Photographed in June this picture leads us into the summer period at Westonbirt. There are currently 82 champion trees at Westonbirt.

Above: Maple canopy

Above: Old Arboretum

Below: Douglas fir and maples on Main Drive, Old Arboretum

Above: In Victory Glade two varieties of the Indian bean tree sit alongside each other with the slower growing 'Aurea' on the right

Left: Betony, also known as bishopswort

Left: Western hemlock

Above and right: Contorted shapes emphasised by backlighting of the sun, Main Drive, Old Arboretum

Right: A canopy in the Old Arboretum

Left: Indian bean tree, Victory Glade, Old Arboretum

Above: London plane

Below: Douglas fir trees

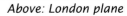

Below: Hydrangea

Below: Foxglove

Named after David Douglas who introduced the Douglas fir into Europe, it is known to have grown to heights of 120 metres in its native habitat of America.

Right: Maple

Above: Maples in the Old Arboretum

Left: Cornus kousa and maple off Main Drive towards Down Gate, Old Arboretum

Above: Beech and holly on Main Drive, Old Arboretum

50

Right: London plane. Mitchell Drive, Old Arboretum

Above: Mock orange

Below and right: London plane, Mitchell Drive

The London plane has an unusual bark that reveals patterns and colours as the bark peels and falls. Its tolerance of pollution means that the London plane is a popular choice for planting in our cities and parklands. The trees can grow rapidly and if left unchecked branches can bend towards the ground and subsequently take root. The shape of the leaves often lead to confusion with maples.

Right: Mock Orange (Philadelphus)

Above: Loop Walk, Old Arboretum

Above: Berberis

Above: A typical Holford View in the Old Arboretum

Above: Mitchell Drive, Old Arboretum

The Old Arboretum is ideal for those who need additional aid to access the site providing level paths and offering electric scooters and manual wheelchairs enabling visitors to explore this area to the full through a network of paths and trails.

Right: Holford Ride, Old Arboretum

Left: Interesting bark patterns

Below: Neillia

Above: Loop Walk, Old Arboretum

The lime green foliage of the Indian bean tree dominates this view of Main Drive. The delicate flowers of Neillia show the beauty of this shrub that was introduced to the UK over a century ago.

Above: Foxgloves

Right and inset:
Indian bean tree
(Catalpa aurea)

*Right: Loop Walk
Old Arboretum*

Above and right: Hypericum, Loop Walk

*Above and right: Along Loop
Walk in the Old Arboretum
many of the hydrangeas are
to be found*

Rhododendron, hydrangea, hypericum and many others
are all here to be enjoyed and admired as you explore
the Old Arboretum and take in the wonderful array of
colour that unfolds before you on your journey.

54

Right: Circular Drive, Old Arboretum

Above: Maples, Circular Drive

Above: Stewartia
Left: Rhododendron

Below: Maple leaves

The burgundy red tips of the otherwise bright green foliage of this maple stands out against the darker backdrop of its neighbours. In these images I have gradually moved in closer to show detail and the effect of the light falling on the leaves.

Above: Lower Downs toward Skilling Gate

Above: Lower Downs
Below: The Great Oak Hall

Below left and right: Picnic path towards Mitchell Drive

Above: Some of the many rhododendrons in the Old Arboretum

Above: Azalea

Above: A green sedum roof with chives on the Maples Restaurant

The detail found in these buds and flowers of the azalea and rhododendron is staggering. The Maples restaurant provides a green roof with chives and other small plants growing on it and an opportunity for visitors to enjoy a drink and a light meal under this canopy.

Left: Rhododendron

57

All: Main Drive and Circular Drive in the Old Arboretum are host to many varieties of azalea and rhododendron with their vibrant colours

*Left: Cedar and Oak,
New Downs Loop by
Dukes Gate*

*Below: Copper beech on
The Downs towards
Skilling Gate*

Above: Birch

*Above: Rhododendron petals carpet the floor
Below: Maple*

Variety is the theme at Westonbirt, be it the wide open
space of The Downs with many of our native trees or
the beauty created by the fallen petals of rhododendron
creating a carpet of soft subtle tones.

Left: Rhododendron

59

All: The childrens' play area near the Visitors Centre is both fun and educational. It's a great hit with many of the visitors to Westonbirt

My granddaughter Hannah certainly enjoys this spot with plenty to explore and learn as well as the opportunity to play.

Above:
Whortleberry

Above: Bamboo on Main Drive, Old Arboretum

Above: Japanese red cedar, Circular Drive, The Old Arboretum

There is plenty of colour and texture to be found as these pictures clearly illustrate, especially the warm tones from the Japanese red cedar and the graduated colours found on many a leaf.

Above and right: Hydrangea

Below: Flowers of the Indian bean tree

Above: Dragonfly

By using macro techniques we can isolate the subject from the background as these hydrangea flowers demonstrate. Also, if you are quick and observant you may see dragonflies especially around the dew pond, but they do not stay still for long. The dew pond can be found near Pool Gate in the Old Arboretum.

Above: Wellingtonia

All: As you walk around Loop Walk in the Old Arboretum you will encounter many colours of hydrangea

63

Above and top centre: Indian chestnut on Loop Walk,
Old Arboretum

You do not have to travel far in the arboretum to enjoy
the spectacle of flowers such as these, they are delicate
in nature, bold in colour and beautiful to look at. Many of
the maples are producing seed heads in a variety of
colours and along with the Indian chestnut found on Loop
Walk offer themselves for visitors to enjoy.

Below: Rhododendron
viscosum

Above and below: Maple seed heads

Above: Mock Orange

Above: Magnolia sieboldii

Left and above: Cornus kousa

Above: Indian bean tree (Catalpa aurea)

Below: Indian bean tree

Below: Hydrangea

Left: Abelia

Above: Common orchid

All of these examples are found within a short walking distance of each other in the Old Arboretum. Two varieties of the Indian Bean Tree (the flowers of which we see on page 56) sit alongside each other on Main Drive and the emerging new leaves are a stark contrast from the more mature leaves. The keen observer will soon discover the common orchid growing often in isolation around the Old Arboretum.

Left: Spindle

Right and below right: Downs Link and the Great Oak Hall

Right: Holford Ride towards open fields

Below: Main Drive Old Arboretum

Right: A shady walk in the Old Arboretum

Right:
Maple

All: Views around Silk Wood

As you explore Silk Wood you will come across the small tree *Ptelea* (often known as the Hop Tree), the leaves, flowers and stems all exude a delicious aromatic fragrance. Wherever you are you can enjoy leafy glades and stunning colours as well as the peace and quiet one would expect from a woodland such as this.

Right: Ptelea, The Link, Silk Wood

All: The fabulous colours of maple leaves abound in the arboretum

You do not have to wait for autumn to arrive to appreciate the lavish display of colour provided by these maples. These photographs were taken in August.

Left: Maple

Below:
Silk Wood

Above: Birch bark

Above: Larch pine

Above: Acorn

For many, the beauty of our trees is found in their shape, but equally their fruits and seed heads are attractive along with the bark of many, such as the striking paper effect of this birch.

Below - Maple on Willesley Drive, Silk Wood

Above left : Japanese maple at Willesley/Broad Drive, Silk Wood
Left: Broad Drive, Silk Wood

These Japanese Maple cultivars with the appearance of three mini mounds provide a striking contrast with the green foliage backdrop provided by their neighbours.

Below: Broad Drive and Willesley Drive, Silk Wood

Above and left: 2000 year old coppice lime, between Broad Drive and Rotary Glade, Silk Wood

Below: Maple

Left and above: Maple in the National Japanese Maple Collection, Silk Wood

Maples abound in a variety of colours, some with very tactile texture that makes you want to stroke them. Near the National Japanese Maple Collection is the coppice lime which has been around for 2000 years on this site in Silk Wood.

71

Left: Management of the woodland around Maple Loop, Silk Wood

Managing and controlling the woodland and undergrowth is an important aspect of the work here at Westonbirt. Much of this clearance work is carried out by a team of volunteers under the expert guidance of a staff member. Even grass cutting is important to ensure visitors are able to access many areas of this woodland and is timed to ensure wildflowers are not disturbed and continue to flourish year on year.

Right: Maple Loop, Silk Wood

Right : Common knapweed

Left: Wild angelica

Above and bottom left:
Viburnum seed head

Wild flowers and seed heads
from shrubs and trees
provide added interest as
you venture along the many
paths and tracks of Silk Wood.

Below: Rosebay willowherb

Above, right and below:
Meadow saffron

Left: A quiet country path in
Silk Wood where wildflowers
abound

Above: Bracken

Meadow saffron, their heads standing proud amidst
the grasslands of Silk Wood, border many of the
grass paths that weave their way through this woodland.

Above: Maple in Silk Wood

Right: Around Silk Wood

Above: Conifers on Broad Drive, Silk Wood

Above and centre top: Monterey pine, Silk Wood

I was attracted to the symmetry of these conifers. The beauty of conifers is that they offer year round colour and texture, require little attention and in most cases are able to withstand the harshest of winters.

Above: Maple, Silk Wood

Below: Holford Pine, Silk Wood

Above: Silk Wood

Left: Sargent's cherry, Broad Drive, Silk Wood

Below: Broad Drive, Silk Wood

All: Broad Drive, Silk Wood

The maples are almost guaranteed to provide colour (albeit changing) throughout the summer and into autumn. Here along Broad Drive we see examples of this as their tinted and tinged leaves stand out against other surrounding trees.

Above: Spiked-leaved maple (Acer Stachophyllum}

Above: Towards Waste Bank, Silk Wood

Close up detail of log piles, bark, seed heads and leaves all provide interesting views of the variety of subjects to be found in Silk Wood.

Above: Sweet chestnut

Left: Westonbirt trees abound with beautiful texture

78

Right: Cherry plum dominates this scene along Main Drive, Old Arboretum

Below: Maple

Already some maples are shedding their leaves and creating an interesting tapestry of colour on the floor below them. Westonbirt provides many opportunities to sit, relax and enjoy the display of colour and form from these and other trees.

Above: Fallen maple leaves
Left: Main Drive, Old Arboretum

79

Above: Golden ash, Pool Link, The Downs
Left: A decaying oak near Mitchell Drive, The Downs

Top left and above: Lebanon cedar, near Pool Link, Old Arboretum

The golden ash contrasts well against the backdrop of the Lebanon cedar, whereas the decaying oak has attracted many a photographer over the years in an attempt to capture it in a variety of moods depending on the seasons and the weather.

Right: Wellingtonia along Mitchell Drive, Old Arboretum

Above: Maple (Acer griseum) at Mitchell Gate Link, Old Arboretum

Above: Along Mitchell Drive

Right: Erman's birch, Mitchell Drive

As you enter Mitchell Drive via Down Gate you have on your left the paperbark maple (Acer griseum), close by is champion tree Erman's birch and opposite a small group of Wellingtonias.

Along Mitchell Drive is the elegantly arched weeping blue atlas cedar (Cedrus atlantica 'Glauca Pendula') with its attractive silvery-blue needles.

*Above: Weeping blue atlas cedar
Mitchell Drive, Old Arboretum*

Below: A carpet of fallen leaves

Left: Oriental plane

Above: Red oak

Above: Snowberry

Above: Cedar

Above: Winged spindle, Mitchell Drive, Old Arboretum

Right: London plane, Mitchell Drive, Old Arboretum

Above: Mitchell Drive towards Morley Ride

The spindle shows the first sign of autumn approaching as its leaves start to change colour. Beyond the arching branches of the London plane we can see the strong colours of the maples standing out against the soft green tones of summer. The black tupelo will come into its own in autumn as its leaves turn a brilliant orange through to red.

Right: Black tupelo

83

Already as you walk around Acer Glade and Specimen Avenue there are signs of autumn approaching as many of the maples are starting to take on their autumnal colours and even on a dull day they brighten the landscape.

All: Between Specimen Avenue and Acer Glade

Right: Maple

84

Above: Decaisnea fargensii

Above: Wingnut

Above: Hawthorn berries

Below: Acer Glade, Old Arboretum

Below: Incense cedar

The fruit of many trees and shrubs begin to mature, the wingnut (*Pterocarya stenoptera*) has long downward pointing wings, the more unusual *Decaisnea fargensii* (blue sausage tree) produces matt blue pods similar to broad beans during a hot summer.

As autumn begins we see the sun lower in the sky and the dappled light brings out something of the magic of Erman's birch and highlights the peeling bark which in itself is one of the attractions of this tree. While tearing the bark of most trees is a sure way to make them die, the birch renews its bark continuously providing an ever changing pattern to admire.

The maples of Acer Glade provide a spectacular display of colour as their leaves take on the autumnal tones that are a major attraction for visitors at this time of year.

All: Autumnal colours around Acer Glade, Old Arboretum

We start to see the longer shadows and dappled patterns created by the lower sun at this time of year. Where the sunlight breaks through we see the floor covered with fallen leaves creating a carpet of brown, orange and red through which many a visitor will walk and kick the leaves.

Above: Mahonia japonica

Left and below: Wellingtonia

Above: Katsura (Cercidiphyllum japonicum), Broad Drive, Silk Wood

Below: Tupelo (Nyssa sylvatica)

Katsura (*Cercidiphyllum japonicum*) is a popular tree with visitors to Westonbirt. An attractive tree in its own right it also exudes a strong scent similar to candy floss. Mahonia produces attractive yellow flowers from late autumn into winter and offers a bright and colourful alternative to the changing leaves.

Above: Harlequin glorybower (Clerodendrum trichotomum)

The clerodendrum produces fragrant white blooms from late summer producing from these rather unusual and attractive fruits in autumn. Equally the seed pods of the magnolia provide an interesting display around the arboretum. We start to see many fungi appearing at this time of year, some growing on old and decaying wood, others pushing rapidly through the woodland floor.

Above and right: Fungi

Below: Hawes

Below and top left: Autumn leaves begin to carpet the ground

Right: Magnolia seed heads

Right: Sargent's cherry

On a dull misty day the maples still bring colour to the arboretum as the picture below shows. We can take advantage of a quiet moment and sit and appreciate the calm and peace such a day brings. Meanwhile in Silk Wood, Sargent's cherry arches out over the autumn scene and the fungi continue their relentless growth producing attractive and colourful displays.

Below: Top of Holford Ride looking towards Westonbirt School

Above: Razor sharp fungus

Below: Stags horn fungus

Left: Acer Glade, Old Arboretum

The red maple leaves have become synonymous with Westonbirt and many visitors will descend at this time of year in an annual pilgrimage to appreciate and marvel at the display that nature provides.

Above and right: Maple

Above: Hawthorn

All: Willesley Drive from Skilling Gate, Silk Wood

A walk through Silk Wood will reward you with a glorious show of autumn colours from our native trees, maples and a variety of others from around the globe. At this time of year the warming sun brings a hint of mist to the air creating a special mood and atmosphere in the woodland.

93

Right and below: Maple leaves

Above: A kaleidoscope of colours and shapes from the autumn leaves

The carpet of leaves provides a colourful display and those leaves will gradually rot and be taken into the soil providing much needed nutrients that promote growth and a healthy soil for future years. In addition, leaf mould also helps to retain moisture, acting almost like a sponge, sub soil with leaf mould is capable of retaining much more water than sub soil without it.

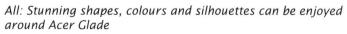

All: Stunning shapes, colours and silhouettes can be enjoyed around Acer Glade

The maples continue with their wonderful exhibition of colour. Colours ranging from yellows through to deep reds are in abundance in Acer Glade and are a feast for our eyes.

All: Spectacular colours are on display throughout Acer Glade, Old Arboretum

Below: Larch in Maple Loop, Silk Wood

All: Maple Loop and Rotary Glade in Silk Wood also share in the glory of autumn colours

Silk Wood can be more subtle in its display of autumn colours and has a character of its own, especially when a misty haze appears created by the warming sun, The Japanese maples mingle below the larch trees and contrast their strong colours against the softer tones of the larch and the undergrowth.

Right: Golden maple (Acer cappadocium 'Aureum')

97

Below: Honey fungus

The yellow and golden hues along Concord Glade bring a brightness to the scene, in contrast a maple stands bare with its leaves lying at its feet while alongside honey fungus mingles with fallen maple leaves.

All: Concord Glade off Willesley Drive, Silk Wood

Glorious golden colours abound in Silk Wood. These scenes are typical of what you might expect to find along Willesley Drive and Concord Glade.

All: Autumn colours and shades found in Concord Glade, off Willesley Drive, Silk Wood

Below: Beech tree on The Downs by Skilling Road

Silk Wood clearly demonstrates it can match any show put on by the Old Arboretum. Enter via Skilling Gate and very soon you will find yourself in the midst of this display of colour.

Above: Willesley Drive, Silk Wood

Top left and right: Concord Glade off Willesley Drive, Silk Wood

Left: Maple

100

All: Majestic trees at the forest shop and Downs Link, Old Arboretum

Long shadows and strong backlighting from the sun emphasise the height of the trees around Downs Link. Visitors are able to enjoy both the beauty of autumn and the various on site facilities provided around the Great Oak Hall.

Maples display their grandeur and beauty in a very special way at this time of year, not just in colour but in shape and form too.

All: Maples in Concord Glade, off Willesley Drive, Silk Wood

Above and left: Maple

Left: A carpet of maple leaves

This is not a view many are able to see, this aerial perspective gives an idea of the density and extent of the arboretum together with the range of colours on offer. The arboretum itself covers an areas of 240 hectares (600 acres).

All: A different perspective of Westonbirt from the air.

All: Westonbirt from the air, showing in particular the visitors and staff complex

From this perspective we can begin to grasp the extent of the provision for parking, visitor services and the buildings and facilities occupied by staff. In addition we are able to see the network of paths that provide easy access to much of the arboretum. Again the rich colours of the maples contrast with the conifers, pines and other trees. Cattle are seen grazing on The Downs close by.

Above: Vistors on The Downs Link near to the Great Oak Hall

Above: Maple leaves backlit by sunlight

The glorious displays provided by the maples quite rightly bring many thousands of visitors to Westonbirt in the autumn to enjoy these beautiful sights and to appreciate the wonder and beauty of nature.

Above and right: Maples catching the sunlight

Above: Maple (Acer griseum). Mitchell Gate

Left: Holford pine

With the right light and weather conditions this decaying oak lends itself to some great photographic opportunities and has presented many a challenge to photographers over the years. The Holford pine (*Pinus holfordania*) arose from a cross developed by Robert Holford and his son.

Left: Oak, The Downs near Mitchell Gate

Above: Maple

Below: Spindle, Mitchell Drive

Above: Erman's birch, Mitchell Drive, Old Arboretum

Erman's birch is starting to take on its autumn yellow, whilst the spindle and maple display their own range of colours throughout autumn.

Lime green tones contrast with the deep reds from a range of maples in Acer Glade. The dark colour of the bark contrasts with the lime green shades and shows clearly the many and varied growth patterns created by these trees.

All: A variety of colours and shapes in maple leaves

Above and left: Maple in autumnal glory

The strong shapes and structure of these trees contrast with the delicate nature of the leaves that drape from their branches in a wonderful array of colours.

The light falls on Acer Glade ensuring the deep reds dominate the scene stealing the glory from those with more subtle and softer colours. Each however adds to the rich tapestry of colour that make Westonbirt the place it is for visitors at this time of year.

Trees along Willesley Avenue in Silk Wood, not wishing to take a back seat, offer up their own contribution to the autumn display at Westonbirt.

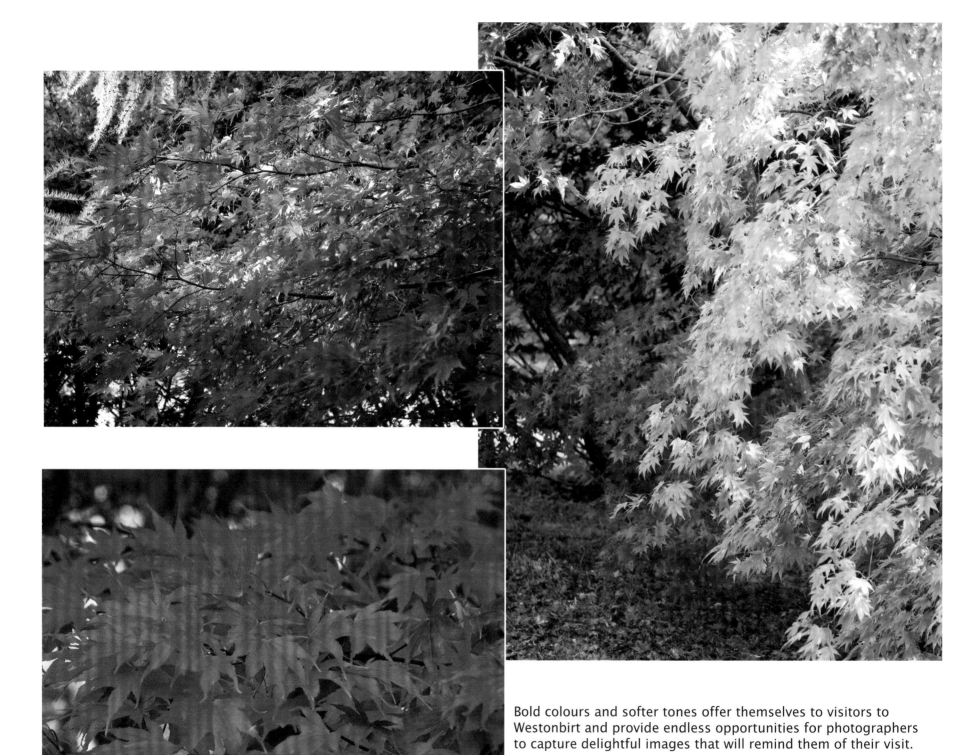

Bold colours and softer tones offer themselves to visitors to Westonbirt and provide endless opportunities for photographers to capture delightful images that will remind them of their visit.

A quiet path takes you through Acer Glade enabling you to view this wonderful display of colour.

Above: Savill Glade, Old Arboretum

Away from Acer Glade autumn takes on another perspective as we see the remains of decaying and dying hydrangea flowers and a carpet of oak leaves along parts of the Old Arboretum.

Above and left: Hydrangea

Above left: Oak leaves on moss

Above: The Downs

Above and left: Oak

The low autumn sun enhances the colours of the beech trees on The Downs. The fresh green of the moss footing the trees contrast with the texture of the bark and the fallen oak leaves, a clear sign that autumn is well and truly with us now.

Above: The Downs

Above: Spindle

All: Autumn views around the arboretum

Whilst many of the trees glory in the light bringing a moody misty atmosphere, the spindle tree glories in its vivid pink seed pods which will later split open to reveal bright orange fruits.

Left: Larch

Above: Fern on the woodland floor

The larch stands tall and erect against a stark landscape whilst ferns are still looking bright and green against the woodland floor carpeted with fallen leaves. Long shadows play on this floor displaying dappled light between the shadows and picking up the texture of undergrowth and decaying leaves.

Above: Lime Avenue, Old Arboretum

Above: Holly

Above: Jackson Avenue, Old Arboretum

At the far eastern end of the Old Arboretum lie Jackson, Lime and Pool Avenues each with their own characteristic style reflected in these autumn scenes. Lime Avenue would earlier in the year played host to bees gathering nectar from the flowers high in the canopy above. Dotted throughout, the hollies display their bright red berries and attractive leaves.

Left: Pool Avenue, Old Arboretum

Left: Fungi

Above, below and right: Loop Walk, Old Arboretum

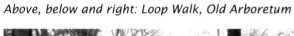

Left: Oyster fungus

Many of the trees off Loop Walk host fungi as numerous varieties appear around this time of year, probably encouraged by the damp atmosphere and right conditions that exist in this area. The strength of the long shadows interspersed by splashes of green from nearby evergreen species offer some indication as to the height and general size of these trees.

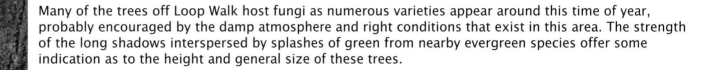

Above: Oak on The Downs near Mitchell Gate

Above: Fungi

These oaks look great on this bright and sunny autumn day with the last remnant of their golden brown leaves just hanging on as long as possible. This iris is nicknamed the stinking iris as its bright green strappy leaves exude a smell when crushed. The seed pods burst open in autumn revealing a string of bright orange berries.

Left: Stinking iris

*All: Autumn sunlight among the maples between
Specimen Avenue and Main Drive, Old Arboretum*

Even though these photographs were taken in
November they show that spectacular colour still
abounds. These particular maples can be found
between Specimen Avenue and Main Drive in the
Old Arboretum. The photographer can take full
advantage of the low sunlight and use it creatively
to produce images similar to these.

Left: Between Specimen Avenue and Main Drive, Old Arboretum

Trade mark maple leaves continue their display off Specimen Avenue well into late autumn providing many opportunities for creative photography.

124

The maples between Main Drive and Specimen Avenue have a particular yellow to golden hue about them as they proffer themselves to the visitor in the latter part of autumn. The lighting breaks through the leaves and canopy of the trees to reveal not just amazing colours but the wonderful form, shape and texture in these trees.

Still in November, Concord Glade in Silk Wood continues with its own display away from the bustle of the Old Arboretum.

Erman's birch, Mitchell Drive, Old Arboretum

Finally winter arrives and we are able to see the whole tree as hoar frost lends a magical tracery to the tips of the twigs. Whilst you feel the cold sinking into you on such an overcast day, this birch comes from far eastern Russia and knows about the cold and reassures us that all will be well as the seasons turn around.

My granddaughter Chloe having fun and finding plenty to play with in Concord Glade, Silk Wood

Left and right: The Downs at dusk

Below: The Great Oak Hall

Below: Downs Link near the car park illuminated for the Enchanted Wood experience

Above: The Forest Shop

Dusk encroaches on The Downs and Westonbirt prepares for the Enchanted Christmas as it lights up a large section of the Old Arboretum during selected days in December.

Left and centre left: The Downs

Autumn is past and the wonder of the colours now stand aside and give way to the thousands of lights that are installed to create magical scenes around the Old Arboretum. The display and lighting effect varies from year to year.

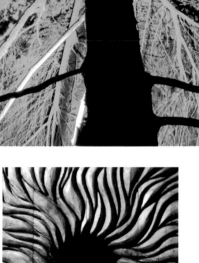

The trees are bathed in light to highlight features and textures around the Old Arboretum. This event attracts vast numbers of visitors each year who are able to enjoy other festive delights including carol singers, Father Christmas, seasonal food and a wonderful atmosphere.

Above: The 'shop window', Old Arboretum

Left: Mitchell Drive, Old Arboretum

Above: Oak on The Downs

Hoar frost accompanied by a misty overcast day creates a special feeling and atmosphere as you walk around the arboretum during the winter months. The lack of foliage enables you to see the shape and form of many of the species.

Above: Dogwood, Holford Ride, Old Arboretum

Above: The Downs Link

Left: The Downs Link

Above: Dogwood, Holford Ride and Pool Avenue junction, Old Arboretum

Whilst the hoar frost brings a different perspective to many of the trees and shrubs, the red dogwood brings that much needed injection of colour to the scene.

133

Above: The Downs Link

Above: Silk Wood from Lower Downs path

Below: The Downs

The Downs are bathed in hoar frost and the ground is hard but this does not deter the moles from busying around and creating a series of mounds on the slopes of The Downs. The trees in Silk Wood bordering the valley take on a magical appeal as they too are draped in hoar frost.

Above and below: Downs Link

Above: New Downs Loop

It may be cold, dull and overcast but the hoar frost adds something to this series of views across the Downs Link.

Left and right: Downs Link

Above: Malus

Above: Holly

Above: Cedar

Above: Hogweed

Above: Snowdrops

Above: Red stemmed cornus

The hoar frost leaves nothing untouched as it rests on many of the common and familiar species. This brings out the creative spirit in the photographer capturing these now attractive looking images. The snowdrops also begin to emerge along Main Drive.

Above: Dew Pond near Pool Gate, Old Arboretum

Winter opens up the landscape as many of the trees are now devoid of foliage. The dew pond is free from the lilies that cover its surface in summer and we are able to marvel at the shapes and textures provided by many of the trees that inhabit this location.

Left: Downs Link

Right: Dogwood near Pool Avenue and Holford Ride, Old Arboretum

Above: Pool Avenue, Old Arboretum

Above: Honeysuckle

Below: Main Drive, Old Arboretum

Above: Off Main Drive, Old Arboretum

Honeysuckle is one of the early flowering species and is accompanied by a wonderful scent. The dogwood stands red and proud whilst families are able to enjoy a gentle winters' stroll through the arboretum.

Right: Downs Link from Main Drive, Old Arboretum

Above and right: Witch hazel

Below: Horse chestnut, Downs Link by the Great Oak Hall

Right: Tree sculpture off Main Drive, Old Arboretum

Witch hazel puts on a display of its spidery flowers and adds a touch of colour to an otherwise dormant winter scene enhanced only by the low strong sunlight with the trees casting long shadows across the landscape.

139

Very quickly rhododendrons, snowdrops and Christmas box burst into flower bringing a touch of glamour to the winter landscape.

Above: Snowdrops, Main Drive, Old Arboretum

Above: Christmas Box

Left and above left: Rhododendron

Above: A resting place, Mitchell Drive

Above: Mitchell Drive, Old Arboretum
Below: Erman's birch, Mitchell Drive

Above: Spindle, Mitchell Drive, Old Arboretum

Left: Mitchell Drive

Snow doesn't fall every year at Westonbirt, when it does it transforms the arboretum into a magical winter wonderland even on a dull day.

Above: Lime Avenue, Old Arboretum

Above: Loop Walk, Old Arboretum

Above: Pool Avenue, Old Arboretum

As snow is blown across the landscape many of the trees take on a layer of snow along the side exposed to the prevailing winds. Meanwhile the dogwood continues to bring a touch of colour to an otherwise monochrome scene.

Above: Dogwood, Pool Avenue

Right: Holford Ride, Old Arboretum

142

Above: Witch hazel

Above: Bamboo

Many of the flowers, emerging buds and leaves are capped with a topping of snow adding contrast with the colour of both flowers and leaves. The snowdrops look perfectly at home.

Above and left: Snowdrops

Below: Rhododendron

Above: Stinking iris

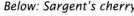
Right: Savill Glade, Old Arboretum

Below: Sargent's cherry

Above: Monkey puzzle

The winter magic continues following a heavier than usual fall of snow.

Above and right: Savill Glade, old Arboretum

Families continue to enjoy Silk Wood covered in snow with its maze of trails, paths and walks. The shape of the trees is clearly defined as they are coated on one side with snow.

Above: Green Lane meets Willesley Drive, Silk Wood

Left and below: Broad Drive, Silk Wood

Silk Wood under a coating of snow provides the visitor with another perspective of this area. Many of the trees stand out against the darker backdrop of evergreens and the dogwood continues to add colour to the landscape.

Above: Waste Gate, Silk Wood

Lead in lines from fencing and pathways plus added features such as gates and seating bring a perspective to these photographs which show The Downs and Silk Wood under a blanket of snow.

Above, centre and below: The Downs from Downs Track

Left: Waste Drive, Silk Wood

Above: Japanese apricot

Above: Rhododendron

Above: Yew

Above: Magnolia

Above: Rhododendron

Above: Cornelian cherry

Above: Rhododendron 'Christmas cheer'

Right: Camellia

The snow disappears and suddenly a riot of colour bursts forth before us in the form of many of the early flowering shrubs and trees that inhabit the arboretum. This reminds us that winter is passing and the prospect of spring is fast approaching.

148

Above and below: Main Drive, Old Arboretum

Below: Pool Avenue, Old Arboretum

Above: From Holford Ride, Old Arboretum

Families enjoy a walk late in winter whilst the sunlight bursts onto the scene. The bare trees at the top end of Holford Ride have their shape and form clearly displayed against the clear blue sky. It will not be long, spring is just around the corner.

Right: Off Loop Walk, Old Arboretum

149

Above: Downs Link

Above: Downs track towards Waste Drive

Above: Bamboo

These views across The Downs bring a feeling of well being as we know winter is on the way out and new life is stirring and preparing to burst forth into spring.

Right: Lower Downs from Downs track

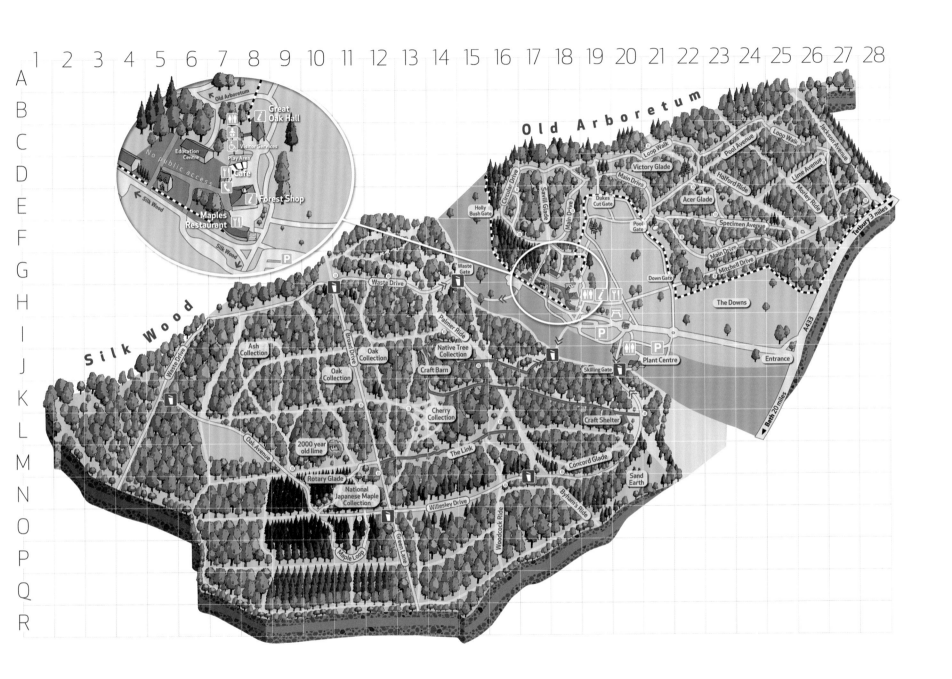

Map reproduced by kind permission of the Forestry Commission.